To my mom and dad who taught me to have courage and determination. To my husband and my daughter, my inspiration.
—MD

For all the kids who feel like the odd one out. As Dr. Seuss said: "Why fit in when you were born to stand out?"
—SD

THE GIRL WHO FIGURED IT OUT

The inspiring true story of wheelchair athlete Minda Dentler becoming an Ironman World Champion

WORDS BY
MINDA DENTLER

sourcebooks
eXplore

PICTURES BY
STEPHANIE DEHENNIN

The full color art was created using Procreate and Photoshop.

Published by Sourcebooks eXplore, an imprint of Sourcebooks Kids

P.O. Box 4410, Naperville, Illinois 60567-4410

(630) 961-3900

sourcebookskids.com

Cataloging-in-Publication Data is on file with the Library of Congress.

Source of Production: Wing King Tong Paper Products Co. Ltd., Shenzhen,
Guangdong Province, China

Date of Production: September 2023

Run Number: 5031136

Printed and bound in China.

WKT 10 9 8 7 6 5 4 3 2 1

I was born in a crowded village near Mumbai, India,
to a poor but loving single mother.

Not long before my first birthday, I became very sick. I couldn't move my legs and my hips had tightened. I was paralyzed.

The doctor told my birth mother I had a disease called polio. He told her I would never walk.

Without money to care for me, my birth mother brought me to an orphanage to put me up for adoption. She prayed another family could give me a better life.

One day, Bruce and Ann Dentler saw my photo and were drawn to my smile. They knew I was meant to be their daughter.

Soon after, I flew to Spokane, Washington, and they adopted me.

My parents taught me to go after my goals, even if they seemed impossible.

"You can do it, Minda," my dad would say. "Just figure it out."

I figured out lots of things that someone like *me* wasn't expected to do.

First, I learned how to walk. After many surgeries on my hips and legs,
at five years old, I was fitted with leg braces and crutches.

Next, I learned how to climb stairs, so I could ride the school bus with my sister.

After that, I learned how to do my chores like my siblings.

It wasn't easy. Sometimes I fell.

Sometimes I got mad.

Sometimes I wanted to give up. But I never did. Afterward, I was stronger, I was smarter, I was more confident!

Even though I could do some things like the other kids, not everyone believed in me, and left me out.

In gym class, I was always picked last or had to sit on the sidelines.

Some adults talked over me because they could only see my disability.

Being different was hard. There were kids who didn't want to be my friend because my skin is dark brown, or because my crutches and leg braces scared them. "The Tin Man," they called me.

But I didn't let those people stop me. I wanted to show everyone what I could do.

I learned how to
play the piano and
performed for crowds.

I worked hard and made the
honor roll every year.

I backpacked through
Europe all by myself.

I even interned at
the White House.

After college graduation,
I got a job in New York City
and got married.

I had done so much, but something was still missing. I was tired of sitting on the sidelines. I wanted to be an athlete. Then one day, everything changed.

In New York City, I joined a running club for people with disabilities.

On my first day, I was loaned a handcycle. Once my feet were set in the foot plates, I cranked the gears and was off!

WHOOSH, WHOOSH, WHOOSH, CLiCK!
WHOOSH, WHOOSH, WHOOSH, CLiCK!
WHOOSH, WHOOSH, WHOOSH, CLiCK!

"Woo-hoo!" I yelled, zooming through Central Park.

I loved cycling, but just like when
I'd learned to walk, I had to practice.
   I made lots of mistakes. I took turns
too fast. I tipped over.

I got stuck going up a hill! None of it stopped me.

Afterward, I was stronger, I was smarter, I was more confident!

A fire had been lit inside and I began competing in races like the New York City Marathon. I felt unstoppable!

I was ready to do a triathlon. There was just one problem. I was afraid of the ocean because I didn't know how to swim.

Then I remembered Dad's words: *You can do it, Minda. Just figure it out.*

I stopped worrying and asked a coach to teach me.

At first, I struggled to breathe and turn my hips,
so I focused on swimming one stroke at a time.

ONE, TWO, THREE, BREATHE... ONE, TWO, THREE, BREATHE... ONE, TWO, THREE, BREATHE...

Afterward, I was stronger, I was smarter, I
was more confident!

I could ride my handcycle for the bike race, but I needed a racing wheelchair for the run. I had never used one before. The bucket seat was uncomfortable, and it was hard to brake. Yet I practiced anyway, pushing the wheelchair up and down the hills of Central Park.

PUSH, PUSH, PUSH, ROLL!

PUSH, PUSH, PUSH, ROLL!

PUSH, PUSH, PUSH, ROLL!

PUSH, PUSH, PUSH, ROLL!

That summer, I crossed the finish
line of the New York City Triathlon,
excited for my next challenge.

I decided to compete in the Ironman Triathlon in Kona, Hawaii. No female wheelchair athlete had ever finished the course. Could I swim, bike, and run 140.6 miles?

Many people didn't think so, but that only made me want it more.

"You can do it, Minda," Dad said. "Just figure it out."

I got back to work and trained harder. Over the next five years, I completed ten triathlons all over the world.

Afterward, I was stronger, I was smarter, I was more confident!

Finally, it was time to compete in my first Ironman World Championship.

When the day of the race arrived, my stomach fluttered with excitement. But from the moment the cannon sounded, all my plans fell apart. I panicked swimming in the ocean. My goggles slipped off. I couldn't keep up with the others.

On the handcycle, my muscles burned, and my throat grew dry. I wasn't moving fast enough. I was not going to make the time limit.

BEEP BEEP! HONK HONK!

TIME KEEPER

As I reached the top of the fifteen-mile hill, I was pulled off the course for being too slow. My race was over. I had failed.

"Maybe I can't do it! Maybe it *is* too hard!" I cried.

I thought about quitting triathlon forever. But my friends and family would not let me.

"Just figure it out, Minda," Dad said. "You always do."

For the next nine months, I swam, biked, and ran more than ever before. I worked with a team of coaches. I ate healthy foods. I lifted weights and I went to bed early. Most of all, I believed in myself.

By the day of the race, I was stronger, I was smarter, I was more confident! And I was *ready*!

On October 12, 2013, I treaded water, waiting for the race to start, along with two thousand other triathletes.

My heart thudded in my chest and my stomach was in tangles, but I couldn't wait to swim.

With a bang, the cannon went off and I burst through the waves. The Pacific Ocean stretched ahead, but like always, I focused on swimming one stroke at a time.

ONE, TWO, THREE, BREATHE... ONE, TWO, THREE, BREATHE... ONE, TWO, THREE, BREATHE...

Then I was onto the bike ride through the scorching hot lava fields.
Cyclists whizzed by, but on my handcycle, I could go fast like them.

WHOOSH, WHOOSH, WHOOSH, CLICK!
WHOOSH, WHOOSH, WHOOSH, CLICK!
WHOOSH, WHOOSH, WHOOSH, CLICK!

After hours of riding, my stomach was in knots and my arms ached. Every bump in the road hurt. I checked the clock and shook my head. There were too many miles to go and not enough time. I wasn't going to make it! *Again!*

"I can do it!" I yelled. "I just need to figure it out!"

I gritted my teeth and cranked the handcycle up the last hill.

"Minda Dentler has made the bike time limit!" the announcer shouted as I rode into the transition with three minutes to spare.

At last, I had reached the final part of the race: a marathon.

I shuffled into my racing wheelchair and was off.

PUSH, PUSH, PUSH, ROLL!

PUSH, PUSH, PUSH, ROLL!

PUSH, PUSH, PUSH, ROLL!

PUSH, PUSH, PUSH, ROLL!

"Whoa!"

The sun had set quickly, covering the road in darkness.

When I reached Palani Drive, my stomach dropped at the sight of the steep half-mile hill.

"You can do it, Minda," I whispered. "Just figure it out."

I gripped the wheels tight and zig-zagged up the hill until I reached the top. Exhausted, I pressed on for the final stretch. I was almost there!

Just a few more pushes and...

TIME 14:39:10

"Minda Dentler, you are an
Ironman!" the announcer shouted
as I crossed the finish line.

I did it! A paralyzed, orphaned little girl from India became the first female wheelchair athlete to complete the Ironman World Championship!

If I could do this, I could do anything!

"I'm so proud of you, Minda!" Dad said. "You never gave up on your goals!"

"Thanks, Dad! I figured it out!"

A Note from Minda

ME

Many said it was impossible. Many said I didn't belong. Many said I should give up. But I didn't listen.

In this book, I am sharing my own journey. My life started as a disabled orphan in India. My legs were paralyzed from polio because I did not have access to the vaccine. I was adopted, moved to America, and eventually became the first female wheelchair athlete to complete the Ironman World Championship triathlon.

With hard work, determination, patience, and a lot of grit, I overcame adversity and failures. I defied the odds and was able to accomplish far more than what was expected of me as a girl with a disability.

Sometimes we may look at other people's stories and think *that couldn't be me* or *I don't have what it takes to achieve big goals*. Going after what we want is not easy!

My story shows you that ordinary people can do extraordinary things—when we are dedicated to making it happen. I refused to quit, and I did not give up. To find the courage and resilience to succeed at whatever it is that motivates us starts with believing in yourself.

I wrote this story for my daughter, but also for readers everywhere. I hope to inspire readers of all ages to accept those who are different, and to never give up on yourself or each other as you chase your own goals, no matter the obstacle. And to internalize the words of my dad, "You can do it. Just figure it out." Because you can.

What is polio?

Polio is a disease that attacks the nervous system and can lead to paralysis. Polio mainly affects children under age five. While there is no cure, there is a safe and effective vaccine that prevents polio.

I am on a mission to end polio, the disease I contracted as a baby in India. I am a global health advocate, educating people around the world about the disease.

I have a daughter and was able to get her vaccinated against polio. With just a shot, my daughter will never have to live with paralysis by polio.

Polio once paralyzed more than one thousand children worldwide every day in 1988. Since then, more than 2.5 billion children have been immunized against polio and the world is closer than ever to ending the disease. Despite this incredible progress, we must work hard to ensure every child has access to the lifesaving polio vaccine.

To learn more about polio and how you can get involved in ending polio for good, visit endpolio.org.

What is the Ironman World Championship?

Judy and John Collins organized the first Ironman triathlon in Oahu, Hawaii, in 1978, with the goal of creating a race for endurance athletes. The winner of a 2.4-mile swim, 112-mile bike ride, and 26.2-mile run was called an "Ironman."

In 1981, the race moved to Kona, Hawaii, and later became known as the "Ironman World Championship." With its legendary race conditions, grueling length, and TV coverage, it is known as one of the most difficult single-day endurance sporting events in the world.

What kind of adaptive equipment can some people with physical disabilities use to bike and run?

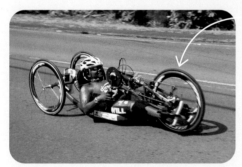

Handcycle

A handcycle is a bicycle that is powered by the arms rather than the legs. Also known as a handbike, it is a three-wheeled device with two coasting rear wheels and one steerable front wheel with gears and crank arms. I use a handcycle intended for racing.

Racing Wheelchair

A racing wheelchair is very different from an everyday one. It is specifically designed to go fast. It features two large wheels on the sides and one smaller one in the front. It is powered by pushing the wheelchair rims forward with your hands. Racers wear special racing gloves, too.

Photos courtesy of Minda Dentler